Heavy snowfall often leads to spring flooding

Floods

Jill Kalz

A+

Smart Apple Media

COPYRIGHT

Published by Smart Apple Media

1980 Lookout Drive, North Mankato, MN 56003

Designed by Rita Marshall

Copyright © 2002 Smart Apple Media. International copyright reserved in all countries. No part of this book may be reproduced in any form without written permission from the publisher.

Printed in the United States of America

Photographs by Sally Myers, Tom Myers, Photri (Will Quinn), Tom Stack & Associates (Dominique Braud, J. Lotter Gurling, Spencer Swanger)

Library of Congress Cataloging-in-Publication Data

Kalz, Jill. Floods / by Jill Kalz. p. cm. — (Natural disasters series)

Includes bibliographical references (p.).

ISBN 1-58340-125-3

1. Floods—Juvenile literature. [1. Floods.] I. Title. II. Series.

GB1399 .K35 2001   363.34'93—dc21   00-052647

First Edition 9 8 7 6 5 4 3 2 1

Floods

Forces of Nature   6

Flood Prevention   12

How Floods Develop   14

After the Flood   18

Hands On: How Different Soils Absorb Water   22

Additional Information   24

CONTENTS

Forces of Nature

They can crush cars. Move boulders measuring 10 feet (3 m) across. Force millions of people from their homes, and kill millions more. What are these tremendous forces of nature? Floods. ⟿ Floods happen when a stream, river, or lake overflows its banks. Floods are the world's number one weather-related killer. Each year, more people die because of floods than hurricanes, tornadoes, or windstorms. And they can happen anywhere, anytime. ⟿ Not all floods are alike.

Roadways can be destroyed by floods

Some floods develop slowly. This gives people time to protect themselves and their homes. River floods can build over several hours or days. Even a lake can flood, but it usually happens over months. Normally, when it rains, the ground absorbs water like a sponge. The water then drains into a river or stream and is carried away. But sometimes there is too much water. A series of thunderstorms dumps rain in one place. Snow melts and spring rain falls. The soil becomes **saturated**. It cannot hold any more water. Rivers fill

Floods are the second most common natural disaster; fires are number one.

up and overflow their banks. This is what happened during the

Great Mississippi River Flood of 1927. The Mississippi

River runs from Minnesota to the Gulf of Mexico. It carries

Rivers can swell and become dangerous

Floods can devastate cities of any size

water from thousands of **tributaries** across 31 states. When

the Mississippi overflowed, it forced more than 600,000 peo-

ple from their homes and killed 246. In some places, the river

grew to 80 miles (129 km) wide!

Flood Prevention

After this flood, the world's longest system of levees

was built along the river. Levees are walls that help keep rivers

from flooding. During the Great Flood of 1993, however, many

of the levees failed. The river was too high. Water covered parts

of nine states and lasted three months. The flood destroyed

more than 75 river towns from Minnesota to Missouri. Many

people lost everything. Forty-eight people died.

Sometimes high rivers break through levees

How Floods Develop

River floods develop slowly. But flash floods can happen in minutes—sometimes without any warning at all. And they always happen near rivers and streams. Heavy rains and dam breaks are usually the causes of flash floods. Areas with sandy, dry soil are more likely to see flash floods. This kind of soil does not absorb water well. Any heavy rain quickly collects in rivers and rushes downstream.

A flood watch means it is possible; a flood warning means it is happening.

Heavy rains can cause a flash flood

More than 100 people died in Colorado in the Big Thompson Canyon Flood of 1976. A heavy storm dumped eight inches (20 cm) of rain in one hour! The canyon walls were rock and could not absorb the water. The river quickly overflowed. Without warning, a huge wall of water smashed into campsites downstream. People said the violent flood roared like a jet engine. The deadliest flash flood in U.S. history happened in 1889 when a dam broke. More

Since 1900, floods have killed more than 10,000 people in the United States.

A rescue vehicle driving through floodwaters

than 2,200 people died when a wall of water 23 feet (7 m) high hit the town of Johnstown, Pennsylvania. But water does not have to be that high to be dangerous. A person can be swept away by just six inches (15 cm) of moving water. Two feet (60 cm) of water can carry a bus. Many people who are killed in floods die in their cars trying to cross flooded roads or outrun oncoming water.

After the Flood

Floods cause a great deal of damage, but they also do

When floodwaters recede, they often leave mud behind

some good. The Nile River in Egypt floods every year. When the water **recedes**, a rich layer of soil remains on each side of the river. Farmers plant their crops in this soil. Floods can give some areas a fresh start. People may move farther away from the water because of a flood and return the land to its natural state. New plants and animal life will move in.

Many cultures believe a great flood once covered the entire earth.

Floods can also bring people and communities together. People may gather together to clean up, to tell stories, and to share food and supplies. For thousands of years, people have

lived near rivers, streams, and lakes for food and water, transportation, energy, and fun. But living close to water can also be dangerous. In minutes, the water can be knocking at your door.

Floods don't last forever

How Different Soils Absorb Water

Some kinds of soil absorb water well. Others do not. Flash floods are most likely to happen where water cannot soak into the ground quickly.

What You Need

Two clear glass or plastic cups   Sand
Dirt   Water

What You Do

1. Fill one cup half full with sand. Fill the other cup half full with dirt.
2. Add the same amount of water to each cup.

What You See

Observe how quickly the water soaks into the two soils. Which type of soil absorbs water best? Which type of soil would be more likely to cause a flash flood?

Farm animals can be swept away by floodwaters

INFORMATION

Index

flash floods 14, 16

levees 12

Mississippi River 9, 12

moving water 18

Nile River 20

river floods 8

soil 8, 20, 22

tributaries 12

Words to Know

dam (DAMM)—a wall built across a body of water to control water flow

flash floods (FLASH fludz)—violent overflowing bodies of water that develop very quickly

recedes (re-SEEDS)—moves back

river floods (RI-ver fludz)—overflowing rivers that develop slowly over several hours or days

saturated (SACH-eh-rate-ed)—totally soaked, unable to hold more

tributaries (TRIB-yeh-tair-ees)—streams that flow into a larger stream or river

Read More

Keller, Ellen, and The Weather Channel. *Floods!* New York: Simon & Schuster Children's, 1999.

Kurtz, Jane. *River Friendly, River Wild.* New York: Simon & Schuster Children's, 2000.

Internet Sites

Federal Emergency Management Agency for Kids
http://www.fema.gov/kids/ready.htm

The National Weather Service
http://www.nws.noaa.gov/om/ffbro.htm

The Weather Channel
http://www.weather.com